ONE CANDLE,
ONE MEAL

One Candle, One Meal

A High Schooler's Business Journey

#ATRUEGPA

Hart Main and Craig Main

Total Fusion Press
Strasburg, Ohio

ISBN-10: 1943496021
ISBN-13: 978-1-943496-02-0
Library of Congress Control Number: 2015945562

Published by Total Fusion Press
6475 Cherry Run Rd., Strasburg, OH 44680
www.totalfusionpress.com

Edited by Kara Starcher
Front and back cover author photos by Barb Huff
Back cover candle photo by Preston Tamkin

Published in Association with Total Fusion Ministries, Strasburg, OH.
www.totalfusionministries.org

Printed in the United States of America
24 23 22 21 20 19 18 17 16 15   1 2 3 4 5

TABLE OF CONTENTS

FOREWORD

As the Director of the Center for Entrepreneurship at Saint Louis University and the Senior Adjunct Professor at the #13 ranked Entrepreneurship program in the nation, I am lucky to meet a lot of successful entrepreneurs.

However, because Saint Louis University is a Jesuit university, we gauge success under a different light. We judge it by four simple words — Do Good. Do Well.

It's easy to do good for yourself through financial success. But the exceptional Entrepreneurs do well for the larger society through their good work.

Hart Main falls into the exceptional category, and he has done it at a young age. He has learned what real success is measured by — building a business while helping society.

His manly-scented candles are made inside real soup cans. And the soup that was removed was originally donated to soup kitchens to feed people who need a little extra help.

Even though the national media has reported extensively on

Hart's business acumen, his real success is found in the number of meals he has provided to those that are less fortunate.

Hart practices concepts that we teach all of our Entrepreneurship students. An Entrepreneur needs to have a passion for their business and a passion for giving back. There are millions of ideas, but the real success is in finding a great business opportunity.

A great business opportunity is an idea that solves a pain for many people who are willing to pay for the solution.

You're never too young to be an Entrepreneur or to start a business. This book is a tremendous opportunity for the next generation Entrepreneur to better understand a winning formula from an exceptional teen Entrepreneur that has a passion for Doing Good and Doing Well.

Tim Hayden
Director, Center for Entrepreneurship
John Cook School of Business
Saint Louis University

- *Chapter 1* -

Desire and Passion are Two Different Things

*"A strong passion for any object will insure success,
for the desire of the end will point out the means."*
– William Hazlitt

In September 2010, on the way to my grandparents' house with my mom and sister, I had an idea that would change my life.

My sister's school started their fall fundraiser, and this year they were selling candles. They sold candles every year, and I thought to myself, "Who in our town needs any more candles?"

My sister, wanting one of the cheap prizes the school was giving away to the best salesperson, was relentlessly trying to get our mom to buy candles. My mom, a candle lover, had enough candles to fill our house with disgusting scents for weeks on end but, nevertheless, wanted more.

"Lavender, Cinnamon, Rose Petals, Beachside." My sister rattled through the scents. I was about ready to puke just thinking of such odors.

"Where's the Bacon, or the Dirt, or even Leather scents?" I asked her. She knew I was making fun of her as I normally do, but I started to think about the matter a little more. "Mom, are there candles for men?"

"I don't know, look it up."

After an hour of searching, I came to the conclusion that no one made candles specifically for men. I thought about it for a little while but was quickly distracted by other things.

A few weeks later, we were on our way home from a youth triathlon where I had done fairly well when I realized that I had gotten my butt kicked in biking by kids with faster, lighter, and more expensive bikes. I was beginning to outgrow my bike and figured it was time for a new one. I asked my parents if they would buy me a new bike that I had been researching, a $1,200 Trek racing bike; the answer was no.

To my parents this was the beginning of a $3,600 purchase because my sister and my younger brother had both started racing triathlons along with me. My parents also felt that if I wanted it badly enough, I could figure out how to pay for it myself. At the time, I was delivering newspapers, about the only job a thirteen year old could get. Since my route was a small route, it only brought in about $75 a month after tips. I knew pretty quickly that paper delivery money wasn't much of an avenue to pay for a $1,200 bike. I did manage to bargain with my dad that he would pay for half the bike if I raised the other half but again that was almost an entire twelve months' worth of saving.

After a few days of thinking of ideas about how to raise money and discussing them with my parents, my mom asked, "What about that candle idea you had?"

Good ideas sometimes start with one issue or one moment. I've had the opportunity to speak with a lot of entrepreneurs, both kids and adults. Almost every one of them can tell you about one moment when the "light bulb" came on or when the idea just clicked; it's hardly ever a long process or a step-by-step process that gets ideas developed.

Thinking back, my mom's question could be the most impactful and time consuming thing that she has said to me. Making candles in our kitchen with my mom was fun in the beginning but got old after a while as most repetitive things do. What made it worthwhile, and still does, is every time I sell a candle I am helping someone both through employment as well as providing a meal. As my business grows, I continue to stick to what has made my business popular and worthwhile to me, sometimes feeding thousands of people every quarter. I had a desire to buy a bike and make candles; I have a passion for helping others.

- Chapter 2 -

Who I Am and Would Become

"No one knows everything,
but everyone knows something."
— Unknown

I was a thirteen-year-old kid who was good at riding bikes, running, playing video games, and remembering sports facts. Some of my neighbor friends even called me "the sports geek." I wasn't exactly the most athletic kid on the block; however, I was passionate about playing sports and had a knack for remembering sports facts. Unfortunately, I didn't know any facts about making candles.

Thankfully, I knew how to use the Internet and knew I would be able to figure out how to make candles. So, I went back to searching. I found a lot of information including stores that sold full candle kits. The kits had everything I would need to make a few candles and included directions and FAQ's. All I needed was to invest some of my money I had made from delivering newspapers, make the candles, and sell them to raise enough money to buy a bike.

My dad reminded me that we had a family friend who had made candles for a while as a side business. I had played baseball with her son a few times, our dads knew each other, so the family would know me if I called and asked for help or advice. I was shy when it came to talking to adults and people I didn't know very well, but my parents really pushed for me to call and gather as much information as I could. So, I called.

The phone conversation lasted about 20 to 30 minutes, and she was very helpful. She suggested a local retailer to sample and purchase scents. She also gave me some tips about cooking in the scent and about how long I would need to cook each batch as well as other key pieces of information. It was a phone call well worth making.

Don't be afraid to ask for help. No one can be an expert in the beginning and especially an expert at everything. Entrepreneurs are almost always willing to give advice to someone starting out or answer questions. They all know how expensive it can be to make a bad decision or how much time it can take to recover from a mistake. Networking with other entrepreneurs is also a great way to make contacts and find out information on other people you can talk to as your business grows. If you're looking for entrepreneurs to talk to, most major cities have groups that meet on a quarterly basis or more frequently. Most of these meetings are during the day when kids are in school so keep summer in mind. You can also do a quick search for people in your field who may be willing to help; you just have to reach out to others.

- Chapter 3 -

Desiring to be Different

"Creativity is just connecting things."
– Steve Jobs

I wanted nothing more than for my candles to be separated and seen differently than those girly scented candles that I despised and to which I was trying to find an alternative. I didn't want my candles in a glass jar or a simple tin like most candles were. Looking back, I never even considered making a pillar candle, so I needed a container.

One evening as I was trying to figure out what container to use, my mom used some soup in our dinner and left the cans on the counter. After considering several containers like pop cans and sport drink containers, I grabbed a soup can and asked, "Why not this? We can eat the soup and then reuse the can."

"That is a good idea," my dad replied. "Guys like chrome, shiny looking things."

We then worked for a while on a label design using a few craft pieces that we had around the house. A few glue dots, some craft paper, and a couple of common office labels that I could run on the printer were all that we needed to create our first label.

> *Make your first prototype or even your first real product out of things that are easy to get and inexpensive. The chances that you will change it as your product grows are pretty good, so don't go into debt making something that you may never sell or will have to change before the final product is chosen. Changing your product can be very time consuming and sometimes expensive, so a prototype does need to be made.*

I have been very fortunate to meet a lot of people who have been very successful in what they do. One of these people is Jim McKelvey, the cofounder of Square. His company is very well known for creating the ability to run credit card transactions on iPhones, iPads, and Android smartphones and tablets. In a speech that I had the privilege of hearing, he said he spent $50 on parts from Radio Shack to make his first working prototype. At the time I heard him speak, his company was worth over $4 billion. One of his messages to the teens he was speaking to was to not let a lack of funds kill your dreams; there is always a way.

The truth is that I made my first 30,000 or so ManCans exactly like my first design using those same original, easy-to-find parts. When I decided to change to a vinyl label, to save time and money, I was concerned it would affect my sales; would my customers like the change? Changing a successful product is pretty scary! After making the change, I recall only one Facebook post from someone saying they didn't like having something that looks like it came from a factory.

Once we started using the vinyl label, I wished we would have switched 20,000 cans earlier. It was such a huge time saver, the product was much more consistent, and it saved money producing the candle. I was pretty frugal with the rest of my business though. When starting my business, I used a Google Sites page (free), soup cans that my parents had bought (free), did a commercial on YouTube (free), and had my mom, dad, brother, sister, aunts and uncles help with the manufacturing (free other than buying a few pizzas!).

- Chapter 4 -

Starting Production

*"You can't build a reputation
on what you are going to do."*
– Henry Ford

After making my list of the manliest scents that I could think of and then researching the Internet to find these scents at the local candle supply store, my mom and I made a trip to buy the necessary supplies. I spent about $100 of my own money that I had made from delivering papers. I purchased an 8 lb wax melter, wax, wicks, color, and my first three scents: Campfire, Fresh Cut Grass, and Leather. I called my leather candle New Mitt. (I still have these three scents available today, and Campfire and Fresh Cut Grass are my bestsellers year after year.)

I started making a few candles with my mom's help. My dad had just finished installing hardwood floors in our kitchen, and mom was concerned that I would spill hot wax on the new floor. As it turned out, the process needed to be closely monitored since the scent has a flash point, which means that if you overheated it, it would start a fire. So, considering my age of thirteen, this part of the process was left to adults.

My 8 lb wax melter normally made twelve candles at one time. We made a few batches, I took some candles to Thanksgiving dinner at my uncle's, and he bought one. My dad took a couple to work and a few of his coworkers bought them as Christmas gifts. I expanded my product line by adding a few more scents like Sawdust, Dirt, and Grandpa's Pipe.

As the word spread, a few more order requests came in. I remember when we advertised on Facebook and my uncle's friend who lived in North Carolina ordered one from me. It was my first out-of-state sale; this sale was a big deal to me at the time.

My family started eating lots of soup, and we began taking bags of soup to our neighbors. They eventually said thanks but no thanks, so we would leave bags on their porches, ring the doorbell, and run. We also started freezing the soup in gallon bags in our chest freezer in the garage. All of our effort was to get the empty can to continue to make candles and sell them.

The Christmas season arrived, and I was feeling pretty good about myself and my little business. Each weekend, my parents and I would spend a few hours making some batches, and the candles would sell during the week. Once the Christmas season was over, I was pretty sure things would slow down.

In mid-December, we went to a craft show at a local school. I thought the craft show would give me a really good feel for how well the candles would be received. I sold several candles that day, and I also got a good feel about how to sell. You can't sit in a chair behind a table and expect people to engage you. You have to stand in front of the table and make eye contact with people as they walk down the hall. When I started making eye contact, it made a big difference in my sales. I also talked to several other vendors about doing this type of show. The show wasn't publicized very well, so not many vendors sold much that day; I may have outsold everyone. At the time, I was selling my candles for $5.00 apiece; the materials were only costing me about half of that per candle, or so I thought.

Product cost is very important to evaluate and understand when you are developing your product. As your business grows, your production costs will hopefully go down because you will be able to buy in bulk, but you may add costs like hiring employees, renting space, paying for insurance, etc. This list could be a hundred items long, so make sure you build profit into the cost of your product up front.

I ended up raising the cost of my candles from $5.00 to $8.00 and then again a few days later to $9.50. When I increased the cost, it was truly a supply and demand issue (which I will talk about later) since the high demand for my product drove up the cost of manufacturing.

You will probably have two different costs, retail and wholesale, for your product. Retail is the cost that your direct customers pay. It is the price you would advertise on your website or sell your product for at a show. The wholesale cost is the price that a store would pay to purchase your product to re-sell in their store. Typically, the wholesale cost includes a minimum number of items that stores must purchase each time, so you lose some profit per item but make up for it on quantity.

How do you determine a wholesale cost? You want your stores to be able to mark the product up 100% and get to your suggested retail price. For example, if I still sold my candles for $5.00, my wholesale cost would be $2.50. The store would then mark the candles up 100% to $5.00. Some products like clothing are marked up 500-800%, so make sure you know your business. Talk to someone who has been there before. As long as you're not competing directly with them, people are happy to help, especially if you can get to someone who is still small and remembers the issues they had getting started. And if you can't get someone to help you with pricing, look at the prices of other products in your niche.

Don't be afraid of making a profit. You may think your profit is large and you don't want to appear greedy, but you will have hidden costs. You will put in more work than you can imagine to have a successful product.

My products didn't exactly fit the retail and wholesale pricing structure because I just didn't know and didn't plan ahead well enough. However, my company mission has become more about feeding those in need than affording a large corporate office.

Also don't underestimate the value of having your product on a store shelf. As long as you have a tag or some type of logo on your product, it's advertising for you 24/7. My candles have always had my web address on them on the center of the label.

After Christmas I made a goal to find a couple of stores that would carry my product. Secretly, my dad thought this would be good for me to see some rejection as things had gone well and came pretty easy up to this point. I put a few candles in a small yellow basket, and we went into town. I had a lot of success in this venture as well. One store agreed to sell them on consignment while another bought my minimum order of 20. At this point, I was selling them for $5.00 apiece to stores as well. A few weeks later, I took the candles to Columbus, Ohio, and went to three or four stores there. The most frustrating part of this process was my dad had to drive me, and since he was there with me, every store owner wanted to talk to him instead of me.

When you're doing sales, you need to have a few things with you. The most important is a rehearsed sales pitch; you can deviate from the pitch, but make sure you stick to the facts. You should also have demo product and a business card with your name, email address, and a phone number on it.

If you don't want to share your cell or home phone number, try using Google voicemail, a free service. The service takes a message, translates the message to text, and leaves the voicemail in your email inbox. This service is perfect for when a call comes in while you're at school or are unavailable. (During school hours or typical business hours is when you will receive most of your calls.) Many small companies use Google voicemail, so it is considered professional; however, make sure you leave a professional greeting on your voicemail.

Chapter 5

My First TV Appearance

*"The business of business is relationships;
the business of life is human connection."*
— Robin S. Sharma

In late February, I came home from school one day and checked the business emails. I read one from a local TV station asking if I wanted to be on a news segment that evening. They had seen my product in one of the local stores that I had sold to just a few weeks before. I called my dad at work, told him about the email, and asked him what I should do. He emphatically told me to email them back and let them know I could be there at any time they needed me. I replied to the email and eventually ended up with a phone call.

Every Friday night, the local sports broadcasters did a short skit before their extended sports segment, and they wanted me to be a part of the skit that night. This opportunity was the perfect experience for me combining product promotion, TV (which I had never been on before), and, the best thing, the sports guys. It couldn't have been better for me. I was very nervous but excited.

My instructions were to come down to the station around 7:00 PM and bring some samples. I had never been through this type of experience before. I expected to show up and be on a very tight timeline with pre-written scripts, have make-up applied, and see all sorts of high-end media stuff. Let's just say over the past few years, I have learned that TV is not as it appears at home.

I showed up promptly at the TV station only to sit and wait in the lobby for fifteen minutes or so. A few people came into the lobby from outside the station and asked what we needed; they were all returning from dinner before the 11:00 news. Eventually, one of the sports guys returned, and we went back to his office. The station was being remodeled, so everything was a mess. All the sports memorabilia was in boxes. I got to go through and hear about all kinds of cool sports stories while we waited on the other sportscaster to get back from the hockey game he was covering. About an hour or so later, he arrived, and it was show time.

We went to the studio, and, to my surprise, these guys had nothing written. They simply had an idea, and they completely made everything up on the spot for the skit. I had one line, "A man in training." Although it wasn't at all what I was expecting, it was a total blast. At the time, I thought I wanted to be a sports broadcaster when I grew up, and the two guys were a ton of fun and very easy going. I did take advantage of the time to ask them about how they became sports broadcasters, what college they went to, their experience, what they look for when hiring someone new, etc.

Because the program was pre-recorded, we ran home to watch. I expected to get a number of orders out of the appearance. Being late February on a Friday night, it was college basketball NCAA tournament time, a great time of year for us sports fans. The second game of the evening went into overtime and pushed all programming back. By the time the game was over and the rest of the news was complete, it was well past midnight so I really don't know how many people saw my segment other than me and my family, but I'm sure it wasn't many. I don't recall if I got any orders out of the spot, but I still had a great time.

Beyond having a great time, the reality of that event was I had met two guys who most everyone in Columbus, Ohio, knew. I have never had to go back to them to ask a favor or try and deal with any promotional stuff, but, the truth is, if I ever needed to, my chances of getting a response from them is so much higher than any other random request because I am sure they would remember me and my product. Even if my request didn't involve the candle business — remember I wanted to be a sports broadcaster at that time — this connection could be huge.

Networking, or making connections in business, is one of the most important things you can do. If you're trying to promote your product or service, develop your product or service, or looking for a job, make sure you make a great first impression. Oh, and my sports segment connection did pay major dividends for me as you will see.

Chapter 6

Investing In The Future

"Someone is sitting in the shade today
because someone planted a tree a long time ago."
— Warren Buffett

Investing may be the one thing that I have found that almost all kids and some adults don't realize is necessary for business. The amount of money that gets dumped back into the business to not only pay for product and labor to create the product but also the amount that needs to be spent on things like product design, taxes, accounting fees, research and design of the next product, rent, utilities, and insurance is surprising. All of these things get paid for out of the profits that your business makes. Yes, it is true you don't pay federal, state, or local taxes if your business doesn't make money, but you still pay sales tax on some things, income tax, payroll tax, etc. Re-investing in your business is why I mentioned in a previous chapter that you need to make sure you build profit into your product. Running a business isn't an inexpensive process. For the entire first year of my business, no one in my family received a paycheck. All the labor was given freely so that I would someday do something great.

At this point, I was still making candles from the house, selling a few through Facebook each week, and selling a few through some local stores. A neighbor who ran a company of his own came over and discussed creating a website with a cart that people could process payments through to simplify things. Currently, we were dealing with everything through email and a very popular online payment system. When someone wanted to buy a candle, they emailed me the order, and I sent them a payment request through the online payment system. Once the customer paid, we shipped the product. The process was long and somewhat time consuming, but, with just a few orders a week, it wasn't that big of a deal. When we looked at the website with a cart, we looked at the hosting fees, the fees for the payment service, and everything that went into it; it just didn't make sense. The website and fees would cost about $30 a month. At $5.00 a candle, my initial product cost, I was making $2.50 profit per candle. If I went the route of the website with the cart, I would have to sell twelve candles before I started to make any money each month. It just wasn't worth it or so I thought. Deciding against the website with the cart saved me money for about two weeks and then cost me thousands.

You should certainly look at every expenditure when you start your business, but keep in mind a few things. What makes you look professional? Where do you want your business to go? Sometimes, actually more often than not, the old saying "You have to spend money to make money" is true.

A lot of people when just starting their business think, "What if this doesn't work out?" or "If I invest my savings, what happens if I don't make money?" I would encourage everyone to answer those questions, but also ask these questions — "What am I going to do next if it succeeds?", "How will I handle growth?", and "If I get a large number of orders, how will I process them?"

Let's say you're going to open an ice cream cart and sell at the local park on just the weekends. What are you going to do if almost every day you operate your cart it sells out? Selling out is a great problem to have, but your cart will only hold so much ice cream. You're missing profits by running out every day, but a second cart will cost you money up front plus a person to run it. There isn't one simple answer to this problem, and there are many ways to fix it. Spend a few moments planning on how you're going to deal with success and grow your business if you're fortunate enough to have this problem. You're starting your business to succeed, not to fail. Have a plan for success.

My goal to buy the $1,200 bike wasn't coming my way very quickly, but I was making money. I actually had $250 in profit when I decided I was going to spend that money on sponsoring my own baseball team. I played summer recreational baseball in my hometown, and my dad was on the board; I knew it was close to sign-up time, and each team needed a sponsor.

"How cool would it be to sponsor the team that I played on?" I thought. Imagine the ManCans logo on the shirt and hat! When else would I have the ability to not only sponsor a team but play on the team that I sponsored?

Be careful where you spend your profits. It's always good to support your local community. Most established businesses use community support to show goodwill to their community as well as gain a tax write off, but 95% of the people don't buy a car at the local dealership because the dealership sponsored a kids' baseball team, but maybe people should. On the other hand, it's never bad to have advertising.

I knew going in that I wasn't going to sell a bunch of candles to parents or kids who played on my team, but I did see it as a once in a lifetime opportunity that I wasn't going to pass up. At that time, I didn't even get the tax write off because I hadn't yet incorporated. The truth is ManCans was more of a craft than a business at the time. Honestly, though, beginning something as a hobby isn't a bad way to start and see if people will buy your product.

- *Chapter 7* -

My First Kitchen Donation

*"A business that makes nothing
but moneyis a poor business."*
— Henry Ford

In mid-February, we began considering the future of ManCans and were definitely realizing we couldn't eat soup forever. Summer would eventually come, and I had plans to sell candles at farmer markets. No one ate soup during the summer. My dad made it very clear to me that we wouldn't buy the soup and throw it away just to get the can; that concept was crazy and wasteful. I agree. People had to be out there who would want the soup and need it.

During the discussions of ways to get more cans, we decided that we could buy the soup, donate it to soup kitchens, and then get the cans back from the kitchens. I was again in a place where I knew nothing about what I needed to know next. I knew nothing about soup kitchens, I knew no one who worked at a soup kitchen, nor did I even know anyone who used a soup kitchen. At that point, I thought it was only homeless people who frequented soup kitchens.

My family started to ask around to see if anyone had a connection to a soup kitchen. My mom came home from work and said that someone she knew at work volunteered at a soup kitchen in Lima, Ohio, and could get us contact information. Once we had that information, we placed a call and set a date to visit on President's Day 2011. I didn't have school that day, so we could drive to the soup kitchen, donate the soup, and bring the empty cans back.

Visiting the soup kitchen was a life changing experience. Kids who were my age and younger along with their families used the services of the soup kitchen. These families were certainly not homeless, so what was a soup kitchen?

I met a few people who worked there plus other volunteers that day. The gentleman who ran the kitchen was Steve. He was exactly what you would think of a man who ran a soup kitchen — very nice and a man of faith. I would get to know him better over the next few years along with several other people whose life's mission is to help those in need. These people each have two qualities in common: they are very strong in their respective faith, and they are very accepting and don't judge others. These qualities are ones that I now try to bring into my own life every day.

Volunteering at the kitchen proved to be a long day but certainly opened my eyes to a world I had never seen before. I had never been hungry, at least not for any length of time, and I had never been in a position that I couldn't do anything about it. I felt like I made a difference in many people's lives that day, at least for one meal.

The above experience isn't much of a business lesson except to say if you have to make a decision about your business and one choice feels right and the other doesn't, it really doesn't matter what the numbers say. Go with your gut. For me, Henry Ford is right— many things make a business valuable other than money.

Chapter 8

Another TV Opportunity

"Not knowing when the dawn will come I open every door."
— Emily Dickinson, The Complete Poems

We donated 250 cans of soup to Our Daily Bread Soup Kitchen in Lima, Ohio. We thought the empty 250 cans would be enough to last us a few months at the rate we were selling candles, but, boy, were we wrong.

A few weeks after we donated the soup, we received a call from a reporter who covered stories for the same station that I had done the skit for with the sportscasters. The reporter wanted to come out to our house and film a segment about my business, and then they found out about the donation. Our house was a mess, full of cans, packing material, and other supplies to make candles. We called one of our local stores and asked permission to film the segment there instead of at our house. The store thought it would be great publicity and agreed to let us film. My parents pulled me out of school for that morning, and we met the news crew at the store in town.

I'm not sure what I was expecting when working with the news, but they sent out the anchor to ask questions and a cameraman to film. They talked about my business, how I had the idea, and why we decided to donate soup. It took over an hour to do the interview and get the shots. They told me it would be on the air that day during the 5:00 PM news. I was pretty excited to be on TV again. For me it was more about just being on TV, not about the marketing opportunity — although, it was a great opportunity too.

The 5:00 PM news came, and I was the last story that they covered, the feel good story that you typically see on the news each night. The story lasted about ninety seconds, and it was uploaded to the TV station website as well. I fielded a few calls from friends, and my parents received some text messages from people they worked with saying they had seen me on TV. We did get a few emails requesting orders from around the Columbus area, so it was a successful day.

A lot of entrepreneurs will tell you that timing is everything. It does make a difference in a lot of situations, but I believe that my product would have been successful any time that I would have created it. It did help that I was a kid, and I would probably not have gotten as much media attention if I were an adult doing the same thing. Media attention really made a difference! Even the media attention that I received that didn't generate sales often generated more attention.

When I launched my product, things were happening in the United States and around the world that really helped focus the need on food for people who needed help.

The country was in a recession, large companies were laying off 1000's of people, and banks weren't lending money to small businesses to expand and create jobs.

Unemployment was at a twenty-year high; Even worse, a housing boom in recent years led to banks lending money to people who really couldn't afford to pay it back, and now that these people were losing their jobs, the banks began foreclosing on the houses. This happened all across the country and caused ripple effects for people who were making their house payments. House values dropped way below what people owed — this term is called "being underwater" or "upside down" on your mortgage.

Then to add to the country's panic, a Tsunami hit the coast of Japan and caused serious damage to nuclear power plants. Everyone on the West Coast was concerned about the power plant damage because the radiation leakage from those units could potentially float across the Pacific and cause issues in the United States.

What I have learned from these disasters is that the media influence is unbelievable in the United States. We follow everything the media says and just can't get enough information about anything and everything. Because of the media's strong influence, any time you have an opportunity for your business or product to be in front of people, do it. It doesn't matter if it is on TV or in a newspaper or magazine; just do it. The opportunity can be a game changer for your business.

Does everything about your product have to be perfect for media attention? No. Remember our house was a mess from producing the candles so we opted for a different venue to showcase our products during the news segment. I have a friend who started a company and was offered an opportunity to be on TV with his product. Just a few days before he was to go on air, he didn't have his website finished and was in the middle of changing his manufacturer, but he still took the opportunity to promote his product to a national audience.

- Chapter 9 -

We're Going to Need More Cans

*"Each problem has hidden in it an opportunity so powerful
that it literally dwarfs the problem.
The greatest success stories were created by people
who recognized a problem [and] turned it into an opportunity."*
— Joseph Sugarman

Watching the 5:00 news segment was great, but then we headed off to swim team practice. If my family can claim anything, it's that we are busy... all the time. We have baseball and softball season, running season and swim season. What this means is that most of the time our time schedule doesn't have room for disruption, and the candle business had been a little bit of disruption up to this point. We were having fun, so we worked around it. My typical schedule was to wake up at 6:15 AM, go to school, come home, deliver the newspapers, go to practice, come home, eat, do homework, and go to bed.

On Tuesday morning, the day after the 5:00 news segment, my parents woke me up just after 5:00 AM and said they had something to show me. I had no idea what they were talking about; sometimes my parents were just weird. Then my mom showed me the ManCans email account on her phone, and she was scrolling through pages and pages of orders. Remember, we had no cart on our website, so getting an actual order and payment was a long process. Four or five orders arrived every minute with two or three or more candles per order. We had no idea why this was happening — only that it didn't appear to be stopping. We couldn't do anything about the orders because I had to go to school and my parents had to go to work. But, before I left for school, we figured out what had happened.

CNN picked up the story that was run on our local news channel the night before and was running it about every hour. Not only did CNN run the story, but also Headline News, plus the Associated Press ran the story in a number of papers across the country. The orders didn't stop! The story was also posted on CNN.com between a story about the nuclear reactors that were damaged by the tsunami in Japan and a story about a family from the United States that survived the tsunami. It appeared that, in a day of darkness for media coverage, they had chosen my story as their bright spot.

The orders continued to roll in throughout the day, but along with the order requests were some emails that I found a little more interesting. Buried in the orders were several interview requests from various facets of media — a couple of radio shows, five or six newspapers, and one or two magazines. Now obviously, like all "good" kids, I wasn't checking my phone at school for texts from my parents (a total lie). Throughout the day they scheduled interviews for me before and after the next couple of days of school. While most kids went home and did homework or played video games, I went home and answered questions from reporters. I spoke with the Toronto Star at 4:00, then Time.com at 4:30, and a local radio station at 5:00. All of these interviews were just generating more orders. This continued for three or four days; and we raised our price of the candle to $8.00. We took a few minutes in between interviews to discuss how to proceed and realized our only option was to fill the orders we could fill with the supplies we had available. We stayed up until 2:00 AM that night, and the next night, and the next… and on… and on… and on. This pattern continued for the next 3 weeks. The best part of this? Waking up at 6:15 the next morning for school.

When I went to school that first day when all of this happened, I had my worst school day ever. Not many of my peers knew about my business yet or the recent coverage. I went to homeroom just like I did every day, and we listened to the morning announcements and watched the daily "CNN for Kids" on the TV in the classroom. This was what we did every day before first period. On this day, CNN covered the Tsunami and the effects on the nuclear reactors, and then the next thing I knew, there I was on TV in front of all my classmates. "CNN for Kids" was running the local news story. When I realized what was going on, I looked down from the TV long enough to realize every kid in my class was staring at me. Not only was my class seeing this story, but the entire school was watching.

The bell rang, and I started walking to first period class. I felt like every kid in the hallway who passed me said, "Hart, we just saw you on TV." This didn't go well for me, the shy quiet kid, but the worst was yet to come. During first period, the teacher picked me first to give my verbal book report. The book report was the farthest thing from my mind. With all of the candle making, I hadn't read the complete book, and I had no ability to focus. The failed book report (really only a C) was the start of my 4.0 GPA downfall.

With the large quantity of orders coming in, my dad took a new approach to the can issue; we thought if we could just buy empty cans from a soup company, we could make candles faster and then just donate some cash to the kitchens. He spent a couple of days at his place of employment, while he was supposed to be working, trying to contact soup companies and can manufacturers. He got a lot of "No, we don't sell directly to consumers." The best offer he received was from one company that was willing to sell us a semi-trailer load, but we knew that wasn't an option we could entertain. The reason we were given this opportunity became very obvious — to feed hundreds of people who needed it. Even at this point in my business, with all the orders we had to fill, I never would have thought it would turn into an opportunity to feed hundreds of thousands of people.

While staying up late working may seem exhausting, and it was, this may have been one of the most valuable experiences I have had. As a business owner, you need to stay in touch with your employees and understand how much work goes into producing the product. Because our order list seemed endless at times, we started making goals. For a while our goal was to not go to bed until the big chair was full of packages to be sent out the next morning. Then we changed our goal to a specific number of packages needing to be done before bed, but we found that we were filling the smaller orders just to get to the end of the day. Goals are very important in a business; make them attainable but also make them so your business grows. Sales goals are a good idea too. Without sales, your business can't grow.

In addition to realizing we needed goals, we realized we couldn't continue making the candles with just our family. Sometimes the need arises to outsource your business.

- Chapter 10 -

More Than One Way to Make a Candle

"Many of life's failures are people who did not realize how close they were to success when they gave up."
— Thomas A. Edison

All of the media coverage and orders caused many supply issues for us plus a huge time issue. We didn't have enough time or room in our house to produce enough candles to meet demand, but we certainly were trying.

The reporter who filmed the original news story that went viral called my mom to see how we were doing. She knew what could potentially happen because of all the coverage. She gave us the name of a man who lived about forty minutes away who owned a candle company and had his own warehouse. She also came back out and did another interview that was shown locally about what had happened to us.

We used the second interview as a ploy for help. We were hoping to get more contacts at places that we could donate soup to. We had already reached out to a couple of local churches, a hospital that ran a Meals on Wheels program, and the kitchen in Lima again. The problem wasn't really finding places to donate the soup, but how to get the cans back and how to get them in the timeframe we needed them. We eliminated all food banks as possible donation sites because those cans would go home with people, and we would never see them again.

We set up an appointment with the man who owned the candle company, and he helped us out with a few good ideas. He suggested cutting down the number of scents that we offered which would help simplify production. At this point we offered between twelve to fifteen scents, and he wanted us to cut back to ten. He also suggested that instead of buying our current scents in gallon jugs that we should switch to his scent producer and purchase scents in twenty- and fifty-pound containers to save money.

Making these changes would mean raising our price again. He told us that anyone who is willing to spend $8.00 isn't going to change their mind at $9.50. So, in a span of a few days, we changed our prices twice almost doubling our original price. Looking back, $9.50 should have been our original price. I don't think it would have made a difference to anyone, and it would have put a lot more money in my business.

We entered into a contract with the candle manufacturer; he had more space, laborers, and the right equipment to create hundreds of candles at a time.

Let's talk about contracts. When someone mentions contracts for businesses, people think of multiple page documents, lawyers, etc. It doesn't have to be that way. We signed a very basic one-page document. The contract stated what each party was responsible to provide and how much my company would be charged to make each candle. We didn't have an end date on this document. The one thing I would suggest for any contract you sign is that you have an out-clause. The clause basically says "in the event that either party isn't satisfied the agreement can be terminated" and then include a timeframe like with thirty days' notice or two weeks. Contracts are tricky but the only time either party refers to them is when an argument arises. Protect your interests, but be fair.

According to our contract, our responsibility was to provide the labels, the paper wrapping for the cans, and, of course, the can. We also had Net 14 terms, meaning we paid the manufacturer every fourteen days for any cans that were shipped. We also paid the shipping charges, which we passed along to the customer.

Also written into our contract was a "dupe" fee. For every scent of candle we wanted the manufacturer to produce, we had to pay over $300 from our previous profits. He told us that he was charged the "dupe" or duplication fee by his scent producer and he passed that cost along to us for our specific candle scents. We later learned, after we brought production back home, that the scent producer had never heard of, and never charged, a "dupe" fee. From a business perspective, I believe that extra work was involved for our manufacturer to begin making our candles, but since he was never charged a "dupe" fee by his scent producer, I feel I was taken advantage of. It's a good idea to ask about charges and see the costs to your partner before entering into an agreement. Looking back on it now, you can say we were the ones who were "duped."

> *I use this story as a warning to aspiring entrepreneurs. While many will truly want to help you succeed, some are just doing it to make a buck off of you. If, as in my case, you are being charged for something that doesn't seem to make sense, look into it. You are entitled to protect your own interests.*

We worked with this contractor for just under two years, and his help allowed us to dig out of the mountain of orders that the CNN coverage, radio interviews, and newspaper articles dumped on us. I thought we had a pretty good relationship with this man, and I even shadowed him for a day as part of my 8th grade career class.

Then one day we received a complaint, and then another, and then another. The downside to having someone else do production for you is the lack of quality control. When we made the candles at home, I was making the candles along with my family's help, and, with our name on the candle, we only wanted the best, which wasn't necessarily the case with our contractor. Over time, we saw a noticeable quality drop in the candles and the shipping process; initially we chalked this up to a change in his production process. We went down to the shop, visited, and suggested he make some changes in order to boost quality. Now, obviously, he was "worried" that he would have to charge us more money.

> *This is where details in our contract would have helped. Eventually, we reached a point where we asked to re-write the contract as we felt it was hard to audit the number of candles being made with the amount of product we were charged for. Our relationship continued to dissolve. We had to find another way.*

- Chapter 11 -

Finding More Kitchens

*"Without commitment, you cannot have depth in anything,
whether it's a relationship, a business or a hobby."*
— Neil Strauss

During the almost two years of outsourcing our production,
we had to find enough kitchens to donate cans to in order to
meet the demands of the orders. Our usual process was to deliver
cans with the soup in them to the kitchen, return home without
the cans, and then go back to the kitchen when the cans were
empty. This process took approximately two to three weeks. When
we returned to pick up the empty cans, we typically took more full
cans, but it didn't always work out to deliver more full cans. Sometimes we couldn't count on receiving every can back in a usable
state since some empty cans would be dented and others rusted.

At the time, we lived just outside of Columbus, Ohio, so we
started hunting locally for kitchens. We found three kitchens in
Columbus and donated to all of them, two on a regular basis. We
reached out to several more within a couple hours of our home.

We also started to hear from friends and family who had connections to kitchens one way or another.

My aunt volunteered through her work at a kitchen in Akron, Ohio, about three hours away from us. We took her some cans to donate, and it worked well. This kitchen was the largest kitchen we had ever worked with, and they had a huge need. They served three meals a day, seven days a week to 250-300 people. It was a perfect solution to our problems — only it was three hours away.

My aunt suggested sending money to her allowing her to buy the soup cans at the same grocery chain as we did and keeping us from having to truck the cans so far. We took that approach, and she was kind enough to clean the cans for us too, or at least tried. What we found was that, although she purchased the cans at the same grocery chain and the labels were identical on the cans, they came from a different plant, and the different plants used different glue. The glue on the cans that we bought locally came off with soap and water; the glue on the cans she bought didn't. A little bit of glue on a can may seem like a small issue, but with the way we had designed the candles, our label didn't cover the entire can. The extra glue needed to be removed. We realized we had to buy every can from our local store and deliver them.

The kitchen in Akron continued to be a goldmine for us. We delivered 2,000 cans at a time to them, and the kitchen would use the cans over a few weeks. Every week, my aunt picked up the empty cans, and we would find ways to transport them back to us. Sometimes my grandpa drove them down to us, and other times my aunt's friend who attended Ohio State University delivered cans to us on the weekends. Our distribution definitely wasn't typical, but it was almost free to do it this way.

We also continued to work with other kitchens. Some of those kitchens were a little trickier to deal with. At times, cans disappeared or would be rusty when returned. So, we were losing cans.

Depending on your business, you will want to consider product losses when setting your prices. If you sell a perishable good, something that may spoil or go bad like food, you may have to throw out product that didn't sell in time. If you're selling clothing, you may have to sell seasonal items at a discount before the season ends. However, consider other ways to make a little from your extra product by donating the excess and taking the tax write-off. All of these things need to be considered when setting pricing and making your plans.

- Chapter 12 -

Bringing It Back

*"I'm convinced that about half of what separates
successful entrepreneurs from the non-successful ones
is pure perseverance."*
— Steve Jobs

After running ManCans from our house for almost six months and then subbing out the manufacturing for about eighteen months and dealing with all the issues that came with that, we decided to take control of the manufacturing and make the candles ourselves. I had reached the point in my business where I had to either make a bigger commitment or shut it down. Making the candles within our house wasn't an option, as that had almost torn our family apart the first time around, and we most definitely weren't going to go through that again. We had a decision to make — do we want to commit to running this business full-time for the foreseeable future or shut down the business?

Previously, we had discussions within the family as to how we wanted this venture to end, and we all agreed the best way would be to, in the future, sell the business. In the meantime, we made the jump and took the next step — finding space for production. The first thing we decided to do was reach out to our local Chamber of Commerce. We were told they would help us find space or, at the least, give some suggestions as what to do.

Most cities have a Chamber of Commerce responsible for bringing business to the town and helping keep business there. Some are very helpful. Ours, however, either didn't understand the size of the business at this point or for whatever reason wasn't ready to help, maybe because I was a kid.

So, we struck out on our own looking for space. We looked again in my hometown without much luck. It was difficult locating a space that had less than 2,000 square feet and was correctly zoned for manufacturing.

Zoning is very important for cities and something you need to be aware of any time you start a business. What zoning does is it divides your town up into sections. Each section is assigned a code or a couple of codes. These codes translate to a definition of what is allowed to exist in this space. It could be residential, retail, manufacturing, or commercial to name a few. Ultimately, what zoning does is it keeps someone from putting a used car lot in the middle of a housing allotment or opening a gas station where the traffic flow would cause a negative impact. These are just a couple of examples, but in the end make sure you know what your business is zoned as before you sign a lease.

A friend of the family who was a postal worker told us about a huge 90,000 square foot warehouse along his route that he knew housed multiple companies. We visited the warehouse, and it was a pretty good deal for us. We could rent 1,000 square feet at a time, and if we needed to expand into the next space, it was available.

Even though the warehouse space had some issues, it was the best we could find. We had a long list of things we needed to make the space work — wax melters, work surfaces, shelving for storage, and some employees to help us. I knew based on the amount of candles we had sold over the past two years that we just weren't going to be able to do all of the work ourselves.

We decided to sign a one-year lease. We chose to do one year so if things went horribly wrong, our commitment wasn't long term. Moving the business necessitated our going to the city and filling out a bunch of paperwork. During that visit, we found out that the facility that we had just signed the lease on wasn't zoned correctly for candle making, although the building just across the street was zoned correctly.

Our only option at that point was to ask the city for a variance. The variance required more paperwork, a $250 non-refundable check, and a visit to a city council meeting for the variance to be considered. At the meeting my dad and I stood in front of the city council members and answered questions about my business. The council members were concerned if we used open flames to melt the wax, if we would be running a store front out of the space, if we would have external signage, if we would be causing traffic issues in that area, and other things like that.

As part of proper procedure, the city council must ask the public (those attending the meeting) for any input before they vote on the issue at hand. A local man spoke up and vouched for my business, not that he knew how we did things but how we were helping the needy and had brought a lot of positive national attention to the town. We were acquainted with the man through baseball; his son and I played on the same team for a year, and our dads stayed in touch over the years. He was at the meeting because he was trying to start a facility offering a number of services to those in need and would actually have a soup kitchen in his facility. His support helped us get the zoning approved for my business to operate in the warehouse.

> *The irony in the situation is the reason we assumed the zoning was correct. We thought we were going to be okay because the building we were renting space in used to be a plastic injection molding facility. But, apparently, melting wax isn't the same as melting plastics.*

Chapter 13

Delivering the News

"Find joy in everything you choose to do.
Every job, relationship, home… it's your responsibility
to love it, or change it."
– Chuck Palahniuk

As business boomed and orders continued to roll in, I spent an hour and a half every day doing what I had spent the last three years doing — delivering newspapers. It seems pretty ridiculous, I know. For the first year of running my business, while using all twenty-four hours in the day to make candles, I used hour twenty-five to make sure the great people of my neighborhood received their local news. It's not that I enjoyed delivering papers; I hated every minute of walking through the snow and rain, but I almost needed that hour of peace and relaxation even if it meant being chased by dogs.

My parents pressured me to quit delivery from day one of starting the candle business, but I couldn't bring myself to stop doing the job that allowed me to start it all. If I hadn't had money from the paper route, ManCans would have gone down as another missed idea. My first job gave me money to invest towards my idea, and I didn't want to let go of that responsibility.

The reason my parents requested I quit the paper is a term called "opportunity cost." We all experience opportunity cost in our lives every day. The paper route was costing me about an hour and a half every day on average. The amount of money I was making in that hour and a half boiled down to just a few dollars an hour. I could use that same time and spend it on the candle business and make considerably more per hour.

I eventually did quit my paper route at my parents' request, but I made sure I gave the newspaper plenty of notice. I even went out and found and recommended a replacement for myself. I left the newspaper, but I did it professionally and on good terms. You never know who you will need to go back to in the future, so I would advise not "burning any bridges."

The local paper covered my story twice, once when we were making candles in my house when I still worked for the paper and then again more than a year later when I had my own space and a few employees helping me. Local papers and regional magazines are always looking for a good, unique story to tell. Don't hesitate to reach out and ask if they would consider covering your business. The worst thing they can say is no. I actually had that happen initially with the local paper that I worked for — they told me no, but once my story hit the national news, they came and asked me for the story.

Chapter 14

Swimming in the Deep End of the Pool

"Only those who will risk going too far
can possibly find out how far one can go."
– T. S. Eliot

Have you heard the phrase "swimming in the deep end of the pool"? The phrase means a few simple things. Swimming in the deep end is risky because you can't touch the bottom of the pool. The second, and most important, meaning is you might as well swim in the deep end of the pool if you're going to swim where you can't touch. Does it really matter if the water is just a few inches too deep to touch or hundreds of feet too deep? If you can't touch and you get tired or something goes wrong, the depth of the water doesn't matter because you're not going to be able to touch anyway.

"Swimming in the deep end of the pool" translates over to business as well. As a business owner, you take risks that could either make you bigger and better (you swim) or it could crush your business (you drown).

The winter before we brought back the production of the candles, a large catalog offered to advertise my business and wanted to sell my candles in their catalog. They distributed over one million catalogs four times a year and had a huge number of repeat buys in their database. My family talked about this opportunity but passed it up because we didn't think we could generate enough empty soup cans to meet their order. Yes, the catalog offer was a big opportunity, but the last thing we wanted was to be back in a situation where we couldn't meet demand.

The following spring, the same catalog company approached us again, and we passed again. The following summer, they suggested just selling online to test the market and the PO was for a few hundred candles. We recognized their offer as a great opportunity, and since they had asked several times and for a large enough quantity that we could keep our pricing the same, we agreed.

A PO is a Purchase Order, which is a contract for one company to purchase something from another. Typically, a PO will list the product, the quantities to be purchased, a price per item, and a total. Also included on the PO are shipping methods, which company is paying for shipping, and terms of payment. The terms of payment are usually Net 10, 15, 30, 60 or 90. What "Net XX" means is the amount of time the company purchas-

ing the items has to pay for the product they receive. Large companies generally choose longer terms like NET 60 or, in other words, 60 days to pay for the goods once they receive them. We negotiated Net 10 terms with the catalog company. For us, a short term was a big deal because, when you manufacture a product, you have money tied up in the product and suppliers to pay that you can't pay until your customer pays you.

The next Christmas, when we were back to manufacturing the candles ourselves again, the catalog company PO was even bigger. They ordered a total of 8,500 candles across several POs from mid-November through a week before Christmas. Between the orders from them, new store orders, existing store re-orders and online sales going through the roof, things were crazy. By mid-December, we were back to three or four days behind in shipping online orders and denying small stores the ability to re-order. My dad spent his days driving soup cans around and picking up empties, and we spent the nights packing candles. I hired a few part-time employees to clean cans, wick the cans, and make candles and labels. It was all very exciting but also exhausting.

At this point, I was going to school, going to swim practice, and then going to the shop almost every single day. When people ask if I miss making the candles, I tell them no. Making the candles ourselves even with a few employees was very stressful to my entire family. My brother who only came to the shop to help once in a great while made his online name for some of his games he played "I hate candles." I really don't miss it.

Looking back, making my own candles, experiencing the demands of keeping up with production, and so much more was priceless. I have friends who own businesses who have never once made their own products after the prototypes were complete. They don't know what the workers go through or deal with when problems arise. I do! I feel I have more of a connection with my product and the people who work for me and work on my product.

As busy as we were, it was hard to sit back and take a look at what I had. I had a business with warehouse and production space. I was providing employment for five people, and, most importantly, providing 25,000 meals a year to those in need in multiple states.

- Chapter 15 -

Hiring Employees

*"Everyone talks about building a relationship with your customer.
I think you build one with your employees first."*
– Angela Ahrendts

When you start your business, wait as long as you can before hiring employees. I say this because it adds another layer of complexity to your business. Once you do hire, spend the time to do it right. When you hire a minimum wage employee with no experience, you get exactly that. I didn't advertise the need for workers; I talked to people I knew in town and let them advertise for me.

The best thing about working for ManCans was the hours were not set. My employees could work whatever hours they wanted during the day or evening as long as the process they were responsible for was finished and didn't hold up the next person in line from doing his or her job. All my employees worked part time, so their hours were flexible for them and us. As demand slowed down, they worked less hours and then added more hours when demand picked up.

My first employee, other than my dad, was a retired man named Hank who lived next to my grandfather. Hank started out cleaning cans, wicking cans, and making the candle. Then at night my Dad and I would go to the warehouse, label the candles, and pack and ship orders. When we would fall behind in production, the rest of my family would pitch in to help at night too. As order demands picked up, the workload and type of work started taking a toll on Hank, and we were staying busy enough to justify another employee.

We reached back out to people we knew and quickly found a friend of the family looking to work during the day when her kids were in school. Sandy took up the candle making process and helped Hank out at times when necessary with wicking and cleaning cans. Next, we hired Debbie and Jonathan to label for us. Adding three employees allowed us to keep a stock of labeled candles on the shelf and, for the most part, we were able to ship orders the next day. At the end of each night, we took inventory and let Sandy know what scents she needed to make the next day.

The best thing about hiring the right person is they make their job better and, in turn, your company better. I didn't have time to figure out the best way to put wicks in a can, but Hank quickly figured out a better way. The new way made his job easier and increased his productivity. When we had made the candles, we would watch the wax turn to solid and then pull the wicks straight so they would stand up. Watching the wax was time consuming, and when you missed it and the wax got too hard, the candle was bad. Hank then took small sticks and wrapped the wicks around them. The sticks were another time consuming process when making a hundred candles at a time but made his job a bit easier. Sandy took those same sticks and added clothespins. Suddenly, we had a much faster process that rarely produced a bad candle. My employees were able to help make the process better and faster and at a very low cost.

I paid all my employees the same hourly wage no matter what they did, and it was above minimum wage. On top of that, we also gave end-of-year bonuses based on the company's profits and the number of hours the employee worked throughout the year. The end-of-year bonus wasn't a guarantee, but something I felt was right to do since they helped me out when I needed it the most.

When hiring people, make sure you know them and can trust them. Once they start working for you, don't forget that they may have some great ideas to help your business succeed. Treat them right, and they will enjoy their work and come through for you when you need them the most.

Also make sure you communicate your vision for your company to your employees and they understand it. My vision was easy. I wanted to provide as many meals as possible to those in need, and my vision was something my employees also enjoyed being a part of so I knew I had the right people.

Chapter 16

Growth Continues

"Growth demands a temporary surrender of security.
It may mean giving up familiar but limiting patterns,
safe but unrewarding work, values no longer believed in,
and relationships that have lost their meaning."
— John C. Maxwell

As my business continued to grow, my grades continued to slip. I was a sophomore in high school and the classes were getting more difficult. Unfortunately, I had less and less time to do homework and study because of my involvement with the candles.

I continued to get free press ranging from magazine articles to talk shows, and the orders continued to roll in. Never once did we have to worry about calling a store back and asking if they needed to reorder candles. We didn't need to since we sold every can we could donate and most of the year we scrambled to meet orders. Looking back, it would have been worth it to do a better job working at connecting with my existing store customers. It's much easier to keep an existing customer happy than to find a new customer and make them happy.

Just after the first Christmas in our new shop, my dad's full-time job laid off a lot of employees, but thankfully he still had a job. A few months went past, and dad decided it was time to start working a little more at ManCans and a little less for his current employer. He started working for ManCans two days a week full-time. He mostly spent his time delivering soup cans and picking up empties. With his additional hours, we reached out to more distant communities more often, increasing not only our donations but also our supply of empty cans.

Between Christmas and New Year's, we had a pretty large profit in the bank. For a business, a large profit means you're going to pay a lot of taxes. Staying profitable has never really been an issue for my company; however, the summers are pretty lean and everything depends on the Christmas season. My dad and I sat down and discussed the number of miles for ManCans he was putting on his personal truck and the possibility of buying a truck for the business. So before I could legally drive, we decided to go truck shopping.

That previous Christmas season, we had sold 800 Corporate Candles to our local Honda dealership. We put their logo along with ours on the candle and worked with the dealership to create the "New Car" scent. Corporate Candles create a perfect relationship. The soup is donated locally to a soup kitchen, then the candle is sold locally, and, in this situation, the Honda dealership donated all the candle sale proceeds to the same local kitchen. Even today, we have continued to partner with other large companies helping them make a difference in their communities through the sales of our Corporate Candle.

We went back to the local Honda dealership looking for a used truck to buy. We had specifics in mind and knew what we could afford. In two days we purchased a company truck... that I couldn't drive.

Sometimes you need to spend money to make money, but you can spend within reason. We bought a very basic used work truck. The truck had a cap on it, something we could use during bad weather without pulling a trailer behind. The previous summer we had purchased an enclosed trailer because empty soup cans don't stay in the back of an open pickup truck very well. Buying the truck also gave me an opportunity to help a local business that had helped me.

Chapter 17

When Your Supply Chain Changes

"Creating a close connection to those you do business with has its many risks, rewards and consequences."
– Mark Cuban

Typically, your supply chain consists of a few vendors that you buy the parts of your product from to make your product. These individuals or companies are very key to your business success, so you want to keep them happy and busy. If one of your vendors goes out of business, it can be devastating, causing a halt in your business until you replace the vendor.

At the time that I operated my own manufacturing facility, I had several vendors. We had a label vendor who not only printed our labels but did almost all of our printing for us — business cards, fundraiser forms, etc. I also had a wax vendor, another vendor that made our scent, plus a number of other vendors that provided services like shipping, insurance, and our Internet service. We also considered the local grocery store a vendor. We bought product from them to make our candles; we just had to donate the soup first.

As we progressed through the year, various things changed with our grocery store vendor. At times the price per can would fluctuate, and other times we had to buy a half case of vegetable soup mixed with a half case of beans and bacon, and other times we didn't. It just depended on how the store received the cans from its supplier. These changes didn't really matter to us. They were changes we had to be aware of, but they weren't devastating. To moderate the price fluctuations, we tried to take advantage of sales when we were purchasing 2,000 to 3,000 cans at a time.

We tended to buy chicken noodle soup, primarily because the can cleaned up easier than a paste soup like tomato. Then one day, the price jumped twenty cents per can. I asked why the price increased so much, and I was told that the price of grain had gone up significantly…that's a head scratcher, but true. Farmers feed grain to the chickens, so when the price of grain skyrocketed, the cost of fresh chicken went up. That price increase trickled down to various chicken products including chicken noodle soup. So as buying fresh chicken became more expensive, the price of soup went up as well. Eventually, the price came back down. Overall, I found the grain and chicken scenario to be an interesting lesson in economics.

We developed a great relationship with our local store. We could phone in orders of hundreds of cases at a time, and the manager would have the cases delivered to the shipping dock at the store; we would show up, load the cases, and pay for them. It was always funny to see the faces of the customers behind me in line when I walked up to the cash register with just one or two cans of soup and was charged hundreds of dollars. The cashiers loved me though because they were reviewed on the number of items they could process in a certain time frame. When I showed up with one can and they charged me for hundreds, they were credited as processing hundreds of items in that time frame.

One day we arrived at the store to pick up our order and noticed that the manufacturer had changed the design of the box that the cans came in. A change in a box is no big deal, but something about it felt different. A few cases into loading the truck, a box broke and some of the cans fell out, not an unusual circumstance. However, I quickly noticed the change in the can too. A barcode had been added to the bottom of the can, and we had seen these barcodes in the past. The barcode was present on other cans that people had donated to us and that my aunt had bought in Akron a few years back.

Entrepreneurs will tell you about their "ah-ha" moment when everything comes together. This was our "oh crap" moment when everything could have fallen apart. I grabbed a can and peeled off the label to find the dreaded sticky glue. The supplier for our local store had changed, and we just purchased a few thousand cans with sticky glue on them. The glue on the cans wasn't going to come off with just soap and water like on the old cans. Our second Christmas season of manufacturing on our own was coming, and this one minor change could potentially impact my company in a large way.

The process of removing the glue on the can instantly became very labor intensive, time intensive, and expensive, none of which my business could really afford during the busy season. We researched a lot of different ways for glue removal, and my employees worked on finding new ways too, but we didn't have much success. I give all the credit to my employees at that time. They worked hard to produce enough cans to get us through the season. The final solution to the sticky can would not only completely change my business again but also help even more people in need.

Having good suppliers is important for the success of your business. You should ask them questions about the product you buy: Do you have more than one supplier? How much of this do you keep in stock? How quickly can you get more if you run out? Do I receive a discount if I order large quantities? You want to ask any questions that may affect your production. Don't worry, asking questions isn't unusual. If your vendor feels like he can't answer your questions or you don't feel comfortable with his answers, you should look for another vendor. A vendor should be looked at as your business partner. The busier your business gets, the more business the vendor will receive. As your business grows, so should the vendor's. If your vendor doesn't have a backup plan, you should. Today, I still rely on multiple vendors and try to keep open lines of communication, making sure the risk of running into issues again is very limited.

Another interesting example of suppliers being interrupted is when my story first aired on CNN. The tsunami that hit Japan affected not only the power plants but also many manufacturers that had facilities close to the shipping ports. There is a major Honda manufacturing plant in what was my hometown in Ohio, and the tsunami greatly affected the plant's supply chain. People in my town assembled cars for a living, and, without parts, the production line stopped. A lot of people worked part time until the issues could be resolved, and a lot of temporary employees were let go making a bad economy even worse for some. Eventually, the manufacturing plant came back online, and things returned to normal, but it took months.

- Chapter 18 -

Another Opportunity to Help

*"Each problem has hidden in it an opportunity so powerful
that it literally dwarfs the problem.
The greatest success stories were created by people who recognized a
problem and turned it into an opportunity."*
— Joseph Sugarman

(When writing this book I didn't realize I chose the same quote
for two different chapters until the editing process. Even with
plenty of time to fix it, I left the quote because I thought it fit
both chapters perfectly.)

Shortly after the first Christmas of doing our own manufacturing, another candle manufacturer, Beaver Creek Candle
Company, contacted us wanting to know if we would be interested in having them manufacture our candles for us. Obviously,
we had been down this road before and it didn't end well. Why
would we ever go down the same road again? Well, they had an
important piece to our puzzle that we couldn't find; they had

the ability to buy the empty can. Although we weren't sold on outsourcing our manufacturing again, it certainly interested us and became even more critical when we could no longer purchase cans that cleaned up easily.

After our initial introduction, we chatted on the phone a time or two and realized that although Beaver Creek's facility was in the same state as us, it was four hours away, meaning a lot of driving back and forth, which didn't seem like a good fit. However, I liked the idea that the company supported a great cause — providing employment for the developmentally disabled who may not be able to find work elsewhere. Eventually, we decided to partner with them to manufacture a second product line that my sister and mom had been wanting me to start, the SheCan.

The Beaver Creek Candle Company was so willing to help us that they actually let us use their top selling scents. Even more amazingly, they bought the lidding machine for the cans, a large financial investment on their part. We realized very quickly that their sole mission was to employ and find work for the developmentally disabled. All of the candles produced at their facility were manufactured by the developmentally disabled. Beaver Creek didn't care about protecting their top selling scents or investing in machinery as long as it provided work for their employees. Our partnership with Beaver Creek Candle Company would eventually flourish and provide a solution that potentially saved my business.

- *Chapter 19* -

Time to Move

"You must take personal responsibility.
You cannot change the circumstances, the seasons,
or the wind, but you can change yourself.
That is something you have charge of."
— Jim Rohn

During the second summer of manufacturing on our own, sales continued to rise, and the process flowed smoothly; however, we still had the sticky can issue. Overall, things looked good for the business.

My mom's job changed a bit that summer, and she started looking for a new place to work. Her needing new employment wasn't a big deal for my business. Then my dad came home with the news that the company he had been employed by for about twelve years and currently worked for three days a week was purchased by a company in Chicago. He had a job until the end of the year. My parents decided that my mom should start looking for work outside of central Ohio; if we were going to move, now was the time. We had no idea what we would do with my business.

My mom quickly found an opportunity to work at a branch of Kent State University in northeastern Ohio. Mom taking a job at Kent State was a great option for the entire family since one of the benefits was that Kent State pays for the tuition of its employees' children. Another plus was our new home would be only an hour away from the Beaver Creek Candle Company. After a lot of thought, we decided we would manufacture our candles for one more Christmas season and would start 2014 with all manufacturing and fulfillment being done at Beaver Creek.

I wasn't really sad about not having to work a ton of hours at the candle shop and into the late evenings during the busy months, but I was sad that I had to tell my employees that they wouldn't have jobs anymore. Most had been there for two years and enjoyed the work and what they were helping me do — feed thousands of people.

The move didn't change my business much from a customer's perspective except shipping happened a little quicker during the busy season. However, it did change things on my end. Since we were no longer donating cans of soup (remember Beaver Creek Candle Company could purchase the empty cans for us), we changed our donation to a cash donation. We decided that since every can of soup cost us around 65 cents to buy, we would donate 75 cents for each candle sold. Over the years, we had seen several times where food donations are highly important to soup kitchens, but money is a greater need. A kitchen that we worked with in Zanesville, Ohio, had a roof leak on Christmas Eve, the night before one of their busiest serving days. Another kitchen had an issue with a gas stove not working. We felt that we could make a greater impact giving the kitchens the option about where to spend the money, whereas donating just soup really limited their options. Moving to a financial donation also opened up the option to donate to food banks which are able to provide more than one meal per dollar donated. Having Beaver Creek on board also helped having a not-for-profit business closely aligned with our business when working with financial donations.

As for me, the move was somewhat difficult. While I wasn't really a people person, I did have friends I had known since elementary school that, up until a few months before, I assumed I would graduate with. On the business side, the first few months were tough, not because of the work load but really the opposite. In the past I came home from school and went to work at the candle shop. Now, I moped around the house for the rest of the evening. I did have work I could do for the business, but it was all online and involved customer service, something I didn't really have a knack for. It was a tough year for me not only trying to adjust to a new city, a new school, and new people, but also trying to re-motivate myself in order to continue running a successful business.

My parents thought it would be a good idea if I got a job over the summer, secretly hoping I would realize how much working 40 hours a week for someone else stinks; they were correct. I realized that, in running a business, I could set my own schedule and decide what I wanted to work on. I slowly began adapting to my new school, making friends, and becoming more involved. While I'm still a very awkward, quiet person, I have benefited tremendously from moving. I'm more social than I ever thought possible, and I feel more a part of my new school and community than I ever did previously.

- Chapter 20 -

Dealing with Failure

"Do not fear mistakes. You will know failure.
Continue to reach out."
— Benjamin Franklin

One of our goals was to visit and volunteer at least one time at every kitchen we donated to. Normal procedure for volunteering at soup kitchens is to show up around 9:30, prepare for lunch, and then work with the regular volunteers to serve the clients who begin arriving around 11:00.

One day when we arrived at a kitchen in Toledo, Ohio, our experience became anything but normal. My dad and I were met by an employee of the kitchen who welcomed us and said if we needed anything she would be in her office. We asked if they had anything else that day to serve other than soup, and she brought out some large party subs that a local grocery store had donated. She left us alone to cut up the sub sandwiches, find the pots and pans, figure out the gas stove, and anything else we needed to prepare for lunch. The kitchen wasn't an area that my dad and I were strong in. Typically, other people did this type of thing for us, but, we knew if people were going to be fed that day, it was up to us. We were very concerned when we realized the lady wasn't in her office and that she truly had left us on our own. Just before lunch started, a few more people showed up to help prepare food and serve, and it ended up being a successful day.

We served about 100 or so people that day, but one man stood out in the crowd. He was an older gentleman who was very loud and argued with one of the servers a lot. The server was a police officer from Toledo, a giant of a man. I am sure the administration had him there in case of any issues with the clients. After we were done serving and helping clean up, the lady who had let us in mentioned it was a shame that the gentleman had regressed. We asked about his story, and this is what she told us:

The man had mental issues but had managed to find a home in a housing complex and get started on medication that helped him with his current state. While living in the housing complex, he decided to plant flowers outside his apartment. Management at the complex removed him for digging up the front yard. At that time, he lost his permanent address and now was back on the streets with no address where he could receive his medication. Sadly, I felt he was probably not the only one in a similar situation.

By the time we met the man in Toledo, we had served hundreds, if not thousands, of people in need, but this one man's story stuck out. In ManCans style, I decided to do something about it.

I started another candle line with part of the profits going towards a non-profit organization to build housing for those with mental and physical disabilities. The new candle line was called Smoke House Candles with all of the scents a different flavor of pipe tobacco. I planned on selling the candles in cigar shops as well as online. The candles were made inside a regular tin, not a soup can, minimizing cost and allowing us to donate more.

After picking the scents, we set up a website and tried contacting a few stores. I didn't get very far. Unfortunately, I found very little demand for pipe tobacco scented candles, no matter how good I thought they smelled. Although I had a great cause to support, I had no one to buy the candles. Most cigar shops sold only odor eliminating candles and weren't interested in our product. I had spent money on design, a website, labels, scents, containers, and even business cards with the Smoke House Logo, all to find the market didn't exist. While not being able to sell any candles was disappointing, even more disappointing wasn't being able to make a difference.

Smoke House Candles taught me a tough lesson, one I was going to learn eventually. Not every idea I have is going to pan out no matter how much money I sink into it. I should have thought a little more about the target market and whether a sustainable level of demand for the product existed. No entrepreneur is successful in every venture, and Smoke House helped me realize that. I still remember this lesson every time I hand someone a business card and they flip it over, see the Smoke House logo, and ask, "Oh, what's this?"

- Chapter 21 -

Great Ideas at Midnight

"Marketing is a contest for people's attention."
– Seth Godin

Throughout the years, I have had several late nights at the candle shop, many of which ended with frustration, exhaustion, and a chocolate milkshake from the all-night corner store. Several instances, however, of working late and growing tired worked in my favor.

One instance was in March 2012. We were once again working late, and I would have rather been many other places, about half of which included watching March Madness in some form. As I sat there monotonously entering address after address into the postal service website, I was thinking about one thing — college basketball. Somehow, in my exhausted brain, I connected basketball to candles and thought, "What if we put our candles in a bracket against each other and make a promotion out of it?"

I sketched out a bracket with the seeds based on candle scent popularity. I took the bracket over to my dad, showed it to him, and explained the idea. He, in a mental state not much better than mine, thought that it was a great idea. Thus, Scent Madness was born.

Over the next few weeks, we posted the brackets on our Facebook page and based the winner on whichever scent had the most orders that week. The winner, of course, was our Fresh Cut Grass, which, in my opinion, is the Duke of Scent Madness. I saw Scent Madness as an opportunity to not only interact with our customers but also add a new scent as well. When I posted a pre-recorded video announcing the winner during halftime of the National Championship game, I also announced our newest scent at the time, Cigar.

> *The campaign appeared to boost our sales a little at the time, and it was a unique opportunity to tie in pop culture with our product. We marketed our product with little to no cost, and it kept the business and numbers fun for me.*

- Chapter 22 -

Independent Youth

"People inspire you, or they drain you - pick them wisely."
– Hans F. Hansen

Because of my business, I have had a few opportunities to travel around the country, and, yes, it is as cool as you may think it is to do this as a teen. My first opportunity came to me by email from a lady who was putting together a group of kids who owned their own businesses, some for-profit and some non-profit. The lady was actually starting her own non-profit called Independent Youth focusing on trying to teach kids to be entrepreneurs through peer mentoring.

I was invited to join this group in St. Louis, Missouri, for a meeting scheduled a month after I received the email. My parents and I talked about it, and we thought it would be, at minimum, a fun trip. We planned to fly in on Saturday, tour St. Louis on Sunday, meet a few kids at a dinner on Sunday night, and on Monday speak to a group of high school kids a few times, and then fly back home. I had spoken to kids before in similar settings, so I wasn't concerned about that part, but it was another missed day of school.

The trip ended up being very fun. Being able to meet other kids that ran their own businesses was, if not a life-changing event for me, an insight into how I looked at my business. I didn't realize until afterwards that not being able to keep up with orders, trying to figure out how to make my business work and fit my schedule, generating enough empty cans, working long hours, feeling the stress it was putting on my family, and trying to keep up with school, was causing a lot of stress personally. I really felt like I was the only kid in the world who was spending all of his free time running his own company.

Even though only three other kids were part of Independent Youth at the time, I enjoyed getting to meet them. One of the biggest differences between these kids and my friends at school was I could talk to these kids about business or, more importantly, how they dealt with business and being a kid. I couldn't talk about business to my friends at school or on my swim team or on my cross-country team. Yes, all my friends asked about the business and how it was going, but they had no ability to give me feedback when I had questions about business. Adults didn't understand the complexity of being a kid, dealing with school, and running a business. So, Independent Youth was a great outlet for me.

I encourage everyone to give his or her own business a try, but it can and will be stressful especially if you're a kid dealing with school and other activities. The busi-

ness lesson here is reach out to others who are in your same situation. Almost every need has a group that you can join either over the Internet or in person. I still belong to Independent Youth, and I am now a Junior Board Member. I see those same kids three or four times a year, and we still have a great time together talking about school, sports, business, and current events. The group has now grown to approximately twenty kids, so I am not the only one.

Chapter 23

Big Time TV

"Things work out best for those who make
the best of how things work out."
— John Wooden

J ust a few months into my business, I realized firsthand what media coverage could do for sales and branding. From that point onward, I took advantage of any opportunity for media coverage.

One day, I received a call from *The Lopez Tonight Show* asking me to come out to the show and talk about my product. I had another chance to travel and this time to Los Angeles, a place I had never visited before. Eventually I would travel back to LA for several shows including twice for *The Jeff Probst Show* and once for a game show on Nickelodeon called *Figure it Out*. All of these shows are no longer on TV. I swear it wasn't me, but what I did learn wasn't only what sells products but also what to expect when you travel for these shows. I got a bit more than I bargained for.

On my first trip to *The Jeff Probst Show,* I was on the show during the first week it aired on national TV. The host did a segment at the end of his show called "Ambush Adventure." This particular segment wasn't scripted, and the host asked me about my business and if it helped me get a girlfriend. During his ambush, he basically made me promise to ask out a girl that I liked in my school. Little did I know that the producers then followed up with my dad to make a bigger deal out of it than it really was. I eventually asked the girl out, and we went out for pizza.

A few weeks later, I planned to head back out to LA for a pre-Oscar awards party, which didn't end up being as cool as it sounds. On the same trip, I made arrangements to make another appearance on *The Jeff Probst Show* to talk about my "Ambush Adventure" and to market my product more. When I arrived at the LA airport, I was trying to find my way through the crowds when a lady came up to me. She stopped only a few inches away from my face and said, "You're that kid, the one I saw on TV. Did you ask the girl out?"

Her comment and question was very out of left field for me. I knew what she was talking about, but it wasn't my focus at that time. After I walked away, I couldn't even remember if I answered her or not; it was kind of creepy. Thankfully, this only happened once, but it gave me a new respect for people who are truly famous and have to deal with fans every time they leave their house.

After working with national TV shows, I learned a few things. Talk shows act very quickly. Producers may tentatively schedule something a few weeks out, but they never book anything until the last minute. One time I had a chance to be on another talk show using a remote live feed from our local TV station. I was bumped from the schedule because a superstar was announcing her divorce after finding her governor husband was cheating on her. That particular TV show opportunity never came back around. However, you can see how quickly things could change. For all of my TV opportunities, we received calls to let us know when to plan our trip, but then received emails later asking if we could fly out within a day or two.

What are the trips like? I'm glad you asked. Typically, these trips include free airfare, but not first class, and a ride from the airport in a nice car to a very nice hotel that is paid for. Majority of the shows will pay for the person they are interviewing and a guardian if that person is under the age of 18. Each show has people who are in charge of getting you to and from the show; they are your contact person or handler. Most of the time, the day you fly in is time on your own and the next day is all about the show.

California has very strict laws about kids on TV and making sure they get their education. I've been told these laws all started after child-star Shirley Temple started making movies and wasn't attending school. When I was on Nickelodeon, my sister, brother, and my other parent flew out on their own. While my brother and sister, who were also missing school, toured the studio campus, I spent four hours sitting in a room with a tutor doing school work.

Not all events are quite as organized as national TV shows. I was asked to speak on a panel of youth entrepreneurs at SXSW, pronounced "South by Southwest." SXSW is a two-week long event that celebrates new music groups, new video production, and new technology. During these two weeks, experts about anything and everything speak as part of a ton of panels. The panel I was a member of consisted of all kids who owned their own businesses. Even though I was fifteen at the time, I was the oldest kid on the panel. This particular opportunity didn't turn out to be much since the panel wasn't very well attended. I did get to spend three days in Austin, Texas, where I had a lot of fun and really loved the city.

Make sure you take opportunities to promote your business, especially when it's free. Also make sure you take the opportunity to have fun. I actually had another opportunity to visit LA for a fun trip to attend the live season finale of "Survivor." Unfortunately, the finale occurred in early December, our busiest and most profitable time of the year. We were making the candles ourselves at the time, so I chose not to go. If the timing is right for a fun trip, go for it. Take the opportunity to relax and relieve some of that business stress.

- Chapter 24 -

Losing Your Luggage in Austin

"An ounce of prevention is worth a pound of cure."
– Benjamin Franklin

When I traveled to Austin, Texas, to speak at SXSW, my dad and I planned to fly in the day before the panel and take a tour of the city, a place I had never been. We flew from Columbus to Phoenix and then to Austin. The flight went as planned, and it wasn't until arriving in Austin that things began to go south (pun intended).

We arrived at the baggage claim and picked up my dad's bag and waited… and waited… and waited for mine; we sat for half an hour before we realized my bag wasn't going to arrive. The airline employees helped us track down my bags which were headed to Las Vegas. Losing my luggage wouldn't have been that big of a deal if we were in Austin for vacation, but I was on a business trip, and I was in sweatpants and a t-shirt, not exactly business attire.

The airline re-routed my bags to Austin and sent them to where we were staying in the middle of the night. Disaster was avoided, and I had my clothes by morning.

I would suggest, on any sort of business trip, to take a carry-on bag with a change of nice clothes if, for some reason, your bags decide to take a trip to Vegas. Other things you will want to consider is flying in the day before you speak or have a meeting; this gives you time not only to relax but to deal with any flight changes or cancellations or, as in my case, lost luggage. Also, place a copy of your presentation on a flash drive and carry it in your pocket. Never check your laptop — always carry it on the plane with you.

Chapter 25

Speaking Engagements

"It's much easier to be convincing if you care about your topic. Figure out what's important to you about your message and speak from the heart."
— Nicholas Boothman

My first experience speaking in front of a crowd was at a local Kiwanis Club meeting during my freshman year of high school. The president of the club knew my dad from coaching baseball and had heard about my business and the charitable work we were doing. He invited me out to talk about starting my business and the donation side of the product. As a fourteen-year-old kid, the only presentations I had done were book reports and other school projects, a far cry from writing and presenting a speech to give in front of twenty or so local adults.

As the presentation date moved closer, I was struggling with writing my presentation and, naturally, was procrastinating. I ended up jotting down some notes on index cards about my business. On the day of the presentation, I simply talked for fifteen minutes about my company, what we do, and why I started it. All in all, it was a successful presentation. The adults were impressed that a fourteen-year-old kid could handle himself so well, and I was impressed I didn't wet myself in front of the crowd.

Shortly after the Kiwanis Club presentation, I had to prepare a thirty-minute presentation for my trip to St. Louis for Independent Youth. At the time, I had no idea how I was going to speak for thirty minutes about my company, but now I have problems telling the entire story in less than that. I still struggle to plan presentations but have vastly improved in confidence and presentation ability.

In the time since my first presentation, I have spoken upwards of twenty-five times about my company with mixed results. I have also watched several other entrepreneurs speak and seen a variety of techniques and skill levels.

While I have spoken many times, at several different venues, only once have I been paid, and that wasn't planned. A local company ordered candles from us to give as gifts to employees following a week-long sales seminar. We offered to hand deliver the candles, and they then asked if I would be willing to talk. I agreed as it offered a good marketing opportunity for my business, and I began preparing an hour-long presentation, the longest talk I had been asked to give.

I arrived at the event very nervous since over fifty business people were in attendance, none of whom I knew, and I wanted to leave a good impression. I went up, was introduced, and dove in. Thankfully, as all in attendance were business minded, I was able to go into detail and just talk about my company, something at which I had become very skilled. I ended up talking for well over an hour and received a standing ovation afterwards. As I was leaving, the owner of the company gave me a check for $250 and thanked me for my time, saying I was one of the best, and youngest, presenters he had heard.

It's important to be able to present yourself well; I attribute my success at this presentation to understanding the audience and their interests. I have spoken several times at local elementary schools in front of hundreds of kids where I have had to simplify the presentation for the sake of the audience. As much as I enjoy presenting in front of younger audiences, I have to rewrite my presentations to make as much of an impact on the listeners as possible. Speaking isn't easy, but, if you know your material and know your audience level, you can do it. It's much different than giving a book report in class; most of the time your audience wants to hear what you have to say.

Chapter 26

Money, Money, Money

"Empty pockets never held anyone back.
Only empty heads and empty hearts can do that."
— Norman Vincent Peale

The number one reason I hear from people why they don't start their own business, especially kids, is because it would cost too much to start or they don't have any money to start one. Go get a job for a little while; not only will you be making money to put towards your startup, but you will be highly motivated to do it as well. Time spent working for someone else isn't a bad thing, but it's nothing like working for yourself.

I challenge you to figure out how much it would cost you to start your own business, and then figure out how to spend only half of that. For example, if you need space and equipment to start your business, look at buying used equipment instead of new. Can you start with a smaller space and work with your landlord to either help with improvements or get the first option on expanding into the space next to you? We were actually fortunate enough that when we rented the 1,000 square feet of space, we could rent the next 1,000 square feet beside us on an "as needed" basis. For two years during the last quarter of each year, we expanded our space allowing us to expand our production during the holiday season; it was a perfect solution for us.

Be creative. Don't let anything, especially money, keep you from being successful.

Chapter 27

Translating My Experiences to Education

"Formal education will make you a living;
self-education will make you a fortune."
— Jim Rohn

When I first decided to write a book, I knew I wanted to teach something. I didn't want to write a "book" that would shove my business down your throat until you bought candles. I have been asked by many people if I have taken any business classes, thinking that I learned something most high school kids haven't in the classroom. Unfortunately, my school district doesn't offer any business specific classes. There were offerings my ninth and tenth grade year, but I wasn't allowed to take any business classes my ninth grade year since I didn't meet the necessary pre-requisites, which apparently didn't include running a business. Ironic, I know. I did take an entrepreneurship class in tenth grade, two years after I started my business. This class, however, was cut the following year because of district budget cuts.

I am saying the above not to complain about the schools I have attended, but to show that you CAN start a business without a business education. You don't need an MBA from Harvard, or really even a high school degree, to start a business. I'm not saying education isn't important, because it is. Education establishes credibility, something incredibly important in the business world. What I am saying is that starting a business will teach you more about yourself and about the world than a high school or even college class ever could. From eighth grade on, I have learned more from a business standpoint than any high school or college class could have ever taught.

One of my favorite quotes is from Mark Twain, "Don't let your schooling interfere with your education." At first, in a world that to an eighth grader appears to be run by your GPA, this was difficult to grasp, but I quickly learned that my business and the knowledge I have gained from it will carry me farther than a 4.0 GPA ever could.